Toutes les illustrations de ce volume sont dues aux photographes
de l'Agence Explorer 70, rue Jean-Bleuzen 92170 VANVES.

A PICTORIAL GUIDE TO

MONT SAINT-MICHEL

C. Paschal

Translated by Lisa Davidson

minerva

A MIRACULOUS VESSEL

AN UNCOMMON DESTINY

Mont-Saint-Michel is a magical site, a picturesque and mystical place that stands between the sea and the Norman pastures. Seen from Tombelaine, Granville, Avranches, Saint-Jean-le-Thomas or Genêts, the ever-changing yet familiar outline of the mount is so breathtaking that it is impossible to doubt the grandeur and genius of man.

The wings of the archangel stand guard over the architectural ensemble constructed on this small granite island, which resembles an immense ship capable of withstanding any storm. Every year, tens of thousands of tourists visit this "wonder of the Western world", which was first a sanctuary, then a fortress and later a prison. The Flamboyant Gothic style forms a coherent unity with the earlier Romanesque architecture. This marvellous stack of buildings, constructed over several centuries, presents an amazing degree of unity and grace; the incredible history of Mont Saint-Michel is recorded in each structure. It was first a pilgrimage site, then became a symbol of power linked to the prestige and authority of the religious order. In 1793, it was converted into a prison, and today, Mont-Saint-Michel, steeped in the illustrious history of France, is one of the most popular tourist destinations in the country.

For Victor Hugo, the Mont-Saint-Michel was more than a wonder of the Western world; it was a world treasure. He considered it to be for France what the Great Pyramid is for Egypt. Maupassant called it a "dream castle"; the Romantics considered it a "sublime thing"; and more recently, UNESCO classified it as a "world cultural heritage" site.

Mont-Saint-Michel seems to rise straight up from the vast sand banks. The spectacular reflections change with every hour and every season.

Left: The image of Mont-Saint-Michel has been reproduced many times. Here, the abbey is depicted in miniature in the *Très Riches Heures du duc de Berry*. Archangel Michael is shown slaying the dragon.
Below: A postcard from the early twentieth century showing beach fishermen on the Bay of Mont-Saint-Michel. Entire families worked on the bay.

Mont-Saint-Michel, like most important historical sites, is steeped in legend and surrounded by mysterious and supernatural events. The legend is inseparable from the history; both have been recorded since the Middle Ages, particularly in a precious manuscript, entitled *Historia Montis Sancti Michaelis volumen majus*, written in the tenth century by a Benedictine monk and kept in the library at Avranches.

The legend of the origins of Mont-Saint-Michel and the role played by Aubert, the bishop of Avranches, mirrors the events which occurred in the sixth century at Monte Gargano in southern Italy. Saint Michael, protector of the town of Siponte, had appeared three times to Bishop Lorenzo while he slept, ordering him to build an oratory in a grotto. When Saint Michael first appeared to Aubert in the eighth century, the bishop, like Lorenzo, waited in order to test the spirits, as he had been taught to do. The third appearance of Saint Michael, in 708, was more remarkable: the archangel's finger penetrated Aubert's head, which finally convinced the holy man to construct an oratory on the island (then known as Mount Tombe). Aubert built a replica of the sanctuary on Monte Gargano.

In 708, the legendary forest of Scissy still covered all the mainland surrounding the two rocky outcroppings; these were Mont Tombella (which became Mont Tombelaine) and Mont Tombe, the future Mont-Saint-Michel. Two hermits lived on Mont Tombe, one in an oratory dedicated to Saint Symphorien, the other in an oratory dedicated to Saint Stephen.

The Sée, the
Sélune and the
Couesnon rivers
flow into
the Bay of
Mont-Saint-Michel.
The Couesnon is
the natural border
between Brittany
and Normandy.

"AT PERIL FROM THE SEA"

Mont-Saint-Michel also has a village — which includes a main street lined with souvenir shops and restaurants (including the Mère Poularde, which serves world-famous omelets) — a town hall, a parish priest, a community of Benedictine monks (who returned in 1966) and a handful of residents who follow the rhythms of the tourist seasons.

Visitors arriving along the causeway from the mainland first discover the southern side of Mont-Saint-Michel. This towering rock, approximately 80 metres high and 900 metres in circumference, is located at the mouth of three rivers: the Sée, the Sélune and the Couesnon. The Couesnon River runs along the west side of the Mont and forms the boundary separating Brittany and Normandy. Tides in this immense bay (40,000 hectares/98,840 acres) can rise and fall by as much as 15 metres. These are

the highest tides in Europe: an outgoing tide can leave up to 18 kilometers of sand banks exposed at the equinox; the sea returns in a mere six hours. These extremes explain the many stories, real or apocryphal, concerning accidents suffered by pilgrims who were surprised by the rising tides; these tides were believed, erroneously, to come in "faster than a galloping horse". The real danger, however, lies in the areas of quicksand which occur at low tide. This unusual and spectacular environment is a perfect backdrop to the exceptional history and architecture of Mont-Saint-Michel itself.

The outgoing tide leaves behind a microscopic chalky-clay deposit, known as *tangue*, a kind of slimy sea-sand that is responsible for the gradual silting up of the bay. It accumulates and is gradually transformed into mud flats which hold the sediments in place; these are the salt meadows where the Blackheaded sheep are pastured. Mont-Saint-Michel is linked to the continent by a 1.8-kilometer-long causeway. It was constructed in five years, from 1874 to 1879. The causeway became the subject of intense debate, which has continued to this day; it is considered to be the cause of the increas-

Left: The cloisters, known as the Jewel of the Merveille, or Marvel, is a suspended garden close to 80 metres above sea level. Completed in 1228 by Raoul de Villedieu, the peaceful cloisters are conducive to the contemplative lives of the monks.
Below: The small columns in the cloisters are unique in that they were not carved in groups of two, as was customary, but in clusters of five.
Following pages: *Le Cloître du mont Saint-Michel,* E. Lansyer, 1881. Note the tricolour enamelled roof tiles designed by the architect Edouard Corroyer; these tiles created an uproar of protest in the Chamber of Deputies.

ing amount of silt in the bay. After it was built, the sea no longer reached the base of the Tour du Roi. A number of projects were proposed to combat this alluvial deposit around the mount. Five teams of architects participated in an international competition in 1991 to reconstruct a causeway that would allow water to flow freely around the mount. In 1995, a major dredging operation was finally approved. This project, which will take seven years to complete, involves replacing one kilometer of the causeway with a bridge that will carry pedestrians and vehicles of residents; visitors will park on the mainland. This project should finally end the threat of a permanent silting up of the bay. The Mont-Saint-Michel will once again be accessible only "at peril from the sea".

Above: The mortars, or Michelettes, taken from the English during their final assault on the abbey, in 1434, during the Hundred Years' War.
Opposite and right: At the beginning of the century, it was still possible to moor a boat at the Mont-Saint-Michel, as illustrated by these old postcards.

A CROSSROADS OF MYTH AND MIRACLES

In ancient times, hilltops were often used as religious sites dedicated to the worship of the sun. Mont Tombe, like Monte Gargano in Italy, has generated a multitude of myths. There are a number of similarities between archangel Michael — a celestial warrior struggling against the forces of evil, personified by the dragon — and the Persian god Mithra, often represented slaying a bull. The Roman god Mercury (a messenger like the archangels), the Greek god Hermes (also a messenger), Apollo (who slew the serpent Python) and Belenus (a Celtic god, son of Gargan) were also associated with the archangel. Aubert, like Lorenzo on Monte Gargano, found a stolen bull on the top of Mont Tombe. The animal was turning in circles around the stake to which he was tethered.

Various views of the neo-Gothic spire on the abbey church. The triumphant archangel at the top rises 155 metres above the sandy bay. It was designed by Victor Petitgrand, architect for the Monuments Historiques, who worked at Mont-Saint-Michel from 1889 to 1898. He was also responsible for the reconstruction of the belfry; his contribution was virtually ignored by a public that was probably more concerned with the ongoing Dreyfus affair.

The bishop understood this to be a sign indicating the exact site of the future sanctuary. He modelled the sanctuary after the oratory in the grotto of Mount Gargano. Many miracles occurred later, often coinciding with various stages in the construction of Mont-Saint-Michel.

At one point, the builders uncovered a megalith they could not dislodge, despite all their attempts to move it. They needed to make a flat surface on which to build the oratory, but they were forced to stop working. Aubert had another vision: the youngest of the twelve sons of a worker named Bain would be able to move the obstacle. With his tiny foot, he pushed the enormous rock to the bottom of the mount, where the bishop's chapel was later built. Once the oratory was finished, Saint Michael instructed the holy man to travel to Monte Gargano and return with some rock and a piece of the red cloak left on the altar of the grotto by Saint Michael. During the trip, the canons charged with bringing back the precious relics observed another miracle when a blind man regained his sight. According to legend, as they neared Mont-Saint-Michel, they were surprised that

Above: Statues of Saint James and Saint Mary. Opposite: After restoration, Saint Michael was returned to the mount on 4 October 1987. The statue of the archangel slaying the dragon had been struck by lightning many times. It was re-gilded and replaced on top of the belfry, which was also restored, less than a century after it was constructed. Following pages: The polders and the mount, viewed from the mainland.

The quicksand has inspired many illustrations and terrifying stories. The risk of sinking into the quicksand has contributed to the myths surrounding the mount — "at peril from the sea" — and the bay. Contrary to popular belief, the tide does not cover the 18 kilometers "as fast as a galloping horse"; it does, however, rise in a mere six hours.

they couldn't find the forest surrounding it. The mount appeared to be encircled by the sea. At the time, this phenomenon was considered to be a direct sign from the all-powerful hand of God (although subsequent explanations propose that this was due to a deforestation of the land during the absence of the canons, as well as to a particularly high tide that carried off much of the vegetation). Aubert formed a community consisting of a few canons dedicated to archangel Michael. The miracles associated with Mont-Saint-Michel continued after the death of the bishop in 725 and the church attracted even more pilgrims. There was, for example, the "miracle on the beach": a woman overtaken by labour pains in the middle of the path leading to Mont-Saint-Michel was protected from the sea by either Saint Michael or the Virgin Mary. Childebert III also knelt before the altar of the bishop, whose ashes had been transported

to Mont-Saint-Michel according to his last wishes. Many invalids were supposedly miraculously healed by his ashes. The reputation of the former Mont Tombe, which had become Mont-Saint-Michel, was established. Charlemagne contributed to the importance of Mont-Saint-Michel by constructing a chateau at Avranches and strengthening the fortifications along the Normandy coast.

ARCHANGEL MICHAEL

In Hebrew, the name "Mikha'el" means "Who is like God?" It was in the name of God that Michael suppressed the uprising of the evil forces against God the Father. The Apocalypse of Saint John describes Michael's struggle against these forces: "A great combat took place in the sky. Michael and his angels fought the dragon and the dragon fought back, supported by his angels, but they were vanquished

and expelled from heaven. The enormous dragon, the poisonous serpent, the devil Satan, the seducer of the entire world was thrown to earth, and his angels with him." The archangel, the celestial arbiter and guardian of the divine order, is represented holding a sword. But he also judges the souls of the dead to determine whether they are worthy of entering heaven; in this capacity, he holds a set of scales. Theologians considered that he held the dual role of *psychopompe*, as he guided souls to heaven, and *psychostase*, because on Judgment Day he was also responsible for measuring the proportion of good and evil in the souls of the deceased. He is therefore both judge and arbiter, preserving the established order against disorder, good against the forces of evil. Pilgrims to Mont-Saint-Michel, particularly during the thirteenth and fourteenth centuries, asked for his assistance against the misfortunes ravaging the country — wars, famines and epidemics — which were generally believed to be the work of the Devil. During the Hundred Years' War, the prevailing image of Saint Michael depicted a warrior bedecked in gold armour. He urged Joan of Arc to take up arms and became her strategist. He was the patron saint of knights, the guardian of legitimacy and protector of kings, their subjects and their realms. Louis XI founded the "Order of Saint Michael" in 1469. In the eyes of believers, the dragon represented the threat of temporal forces. The weak therefore asked the archangel to protect them from calamities, while the powerful expected him to support them against invasions and insurrections.

MONT-SAINT-MICHEL THROUGH THE CENTURIES OR THE HISTORY OF THE LEGEND

FAME

A terrible invasion in the ninth century threatened Mont-Saint-Michel and the surrounding countryside. Men from the north, the Vikings, pillaged a large part of the kingdom; they travelled inland as far as Paris. Mont-Saint-Michel was miraculously spared by the invaders and was used as a refuge by the terrified local villagers, who discovered that the canons were more interested in their own worldly influence than in the powers above.

In 911, the Treaty of Saint-Clair-sur-Epte named Rollon, the Viking leader, as duc de Normandie; in exchange, he converted to Christianity and promised peace. This treaty granted the province and Mont-Saint-Michel to a powerful protector. His descendant, Richard I — known as "the Fearless" and "the Pious" — made several major changes at Mont-Saint-Michel. In 966, he transformed the monastery into a collegiate church; the canons then left and were replaced with Benedictine monks led by Maynard, abbot of the Fontenelle Abbey founded by Saint Wandrille. The Rule of Saint Benedict governed everyday life on the mount. The immense religious faith of the lay population in the year 1000, supported by the many miracles, made Mont-Saint-Michel an exceedingly famous pilgrimage site.

In 1017, Richard II married Judith de Bretagne on Mont-Saint-Michel; he then began to construct the abbey. The weight of the church was supported by large crypts. When the Roman nave, attributed to Hildebert II, was completed, the Aumônerie (Almshouse) was constructed, which supported the Pro-

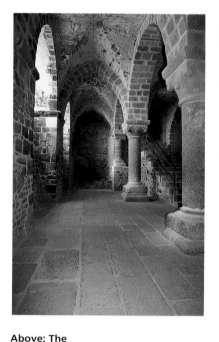

Above: The ribbed-vault construction of the Promenoir des Moines (Monk's Walk). Opposite: The Romanesque section of the abbey church.

Right: The Crypte des Gros Piliers. The enormous columns, 5 metres in circumference, support the abbey church. This crypt, together with two others, Saint-Martin and Notre-Dame-des-Trente-Cierges, form the shape of a cross under the Romanesque part of the church.

Left: The Réfectoire (refectory), situated on the top floor of the Merveille, has a vaulted wooden ceiling and is easily recognised by the many narrow windows. It is situated just above the Salle des Hôtes.

Opposite: The bells of the abbey. The original bells were removed during the Revolution and melted down in Rouen.

menoir des Moines (Monk's Walk) and the Dortoir (Dormitory).

The eleventh century was also marked by the invasion of England by William the Conqueror, who was also duc de Normandie. Mont-Saint-Michel was closely involved with this expedition: the abbey contributed three vessels and four monks, each of whom founded an abbey in the new kingdom. In return, Mont-Saint-Michel received large tracts of property in England. William's historic victory is recorded in the famous Bayeux tapestries, attributed to Queen Mathilda, although it is now believed they were commissioned by Odon, bishop of Bayeux.

An image of Mont-Saint-Michel is embroidered into the work.

After William's death in 1087 the succession of the English-Norman kingdom was seriously contested by his sons Robert Curthose, William Rufus and Henry Beauclerc. The youngest son, Henry, was besieged at Mont-Saint-Michel for some time by his two brothers, but finally gained the upper hand. In 1154, his grandson became King Henry II of England, whose marriage to Eleanor of Aquitaine gave him a vast kingdom extending from Scotland to Spain. This made him one of the most powerful rulers of the time.

Opposite: Flying-buttresses and buttresses on the outside of the Merveille contribute to the beauty of the structure. These elements were essential in the construction of the soaring, pure Flamboyant Gothic chancel in the abbey church.

years he ruled over the monastery (1154-86), he contributed considerably to the development of Mont-Saint-Michel. He reorganised the spiritual life of the monastery and encouraged literary activities. The number of monks increased from thirty to sixty; many of them worked in the *scriptorium*, where copyists, illuminators and parchment makers worked day after day writing, decorating and illustrating the many works which filled the shelves of the library. An inventory taken in 1790, during the Revolution, recorded more than four thousand manuscripts.

Despite the turmoil of history, the abbey remained close to the reigning powers. A group of priors known as the "Lombard clan", were among the king's trusted advisors. They included Guillaume de Volpiano, abbot of Jumièges; Suppo, abbot of Mont-Saint-Michel; Lanfranc, abbot of Saint-Étienne de Caen; Hellouin, abbot of Bec; and Anselm, archbishop of Canterbury.

GRANDEUR AND PROSPERITY

In 1154, Robert de Torigny, prior of the Abbey of Bec, was elected abbot of Mont-Saint-Michel. He was a skilful diplomat and advisor to Henry II, the first Plantagenêt king of England. During the thirty-two

Initially financed by gifts from the many pilgrims who came to Mont-Saint-Michel, the monastery soon became immensely wealthy with the sumptuous gifts and bequests donated by the great lords. By the twelfth century, the abbey owned six baronies, twenty-six priories, seventy-four parishes, vineyards, mills, and land in England, Jersey and Italy. The abbey was at the height of its glory and was able to finance the many construction projects underway. The temporal power of Robert de Torigny was such that he was as influential as many of the princes of his time. A talented politician, he was able to organise a meeting at Mont-Saint-Michel between rivals Henry II and

The summit of the mount is covered with a forest of granite stone. Lower down the hill is a patchwork of grey slate roofs.

Louis VII, which resulted in a temporary peace. He also intervened after the assassination of archbishop Thomas Becket in Canterbury Cathedral, obtaining an agreement from the English monarch, who supposedly ordered the crime, to publicly atone on the steps of the Avranches Cathedral.

Torigny, a brilliant politician, skilful diplomat and prolific writer, was also committed to expanding the existing structures. He was, however, somewhat less successful in these undertakings. Under his "reign", the abbot enlarged the outbuildings; no more than a few traces of this project remain today. The north belfry collapsed in the fourteenth century, the south belfry disappeared in a fire in 1776 and the entire guest house to the south collapsed.

The remains of Robert de Torigny lie under the granite slab washed by the sea air and spray, over which pass the countless visitors to the site. He was one of the most influential figures in creating the grandeur and influence of Mont-Saint-Michel.

PHILIPPE AUGUSTE AND THE "MERVEILLE"

The issue of Henry II's successor arose twenty years after Robert de Torigny's death. It was not a smooth transition; the Plantagenêt dynasty was seriously weakened by the bloody rivalries of his heirs. Philippe Auguste, king of France since 1180, actively participated in the conflicts. He inflamed passions, exploited bitterness and played the role of arbiter, although he was anything but impartial. After the elimination of the first three Plantagenêt sons — Henry the Younger, Geoffroy de Bretagne and Richard the Lionhearted — the French monarch had only to contend with the weak King John (Lackland, or England's Bad King John). In 1204, Normandy once again became part of French territory. Mont-Saint-Michel was the final point of resistance: the residents did not surrender under the assaults of the Breton army commanded by Guy de Thouars; they were finally defeated by an enormous fire that first engulfed the village, then destroyed the abbey. All

that remained were the walls and arches.

In compensation for this sacrilege perpetrated on Mont-Saint-Michel by the Bretons, Philippe Auguste donated an enormous amount of money to reconstruct a series of buildings. The best architects and craftsmen in the kingdom worked for twenty years — a very short time — to create the splendid Gothic structure called "La Merveille" (Marvel) by dazzled pilgrims.

Abbot Jourdain began by constructing the eastern wing of the Merveille; the western wing was completed by his successors. Using materials culled from the old abbey, the craftsmen constructed a cathedral 100 metres long by 40 metres wide. It is unique in that it includes the guest halls, refectory and monastery within its walls. After the collapse of the upper sections of the nave in 1103, the destruction of the buildings by lightning in 1112 and the fires of 1138 and 1204, the

abbey rose once again from its ashes. The fortifications built at the time have protected the site for centuries.

Mont-Saint-Michel was aided by the patronage of successive kings of France: Saint Louis donated a sack of gold, Philippe le Bel gave a piece of the real cross and two thorns from the crown of Christ, and Alexandre IV gave a mitre to the abbot, making him a bishop.

A UNIQUE MONASTERY

The splendid isolation of Mont-Saint-Michel meant that the monks achieved a self-sufficiency which was conducive to the contemplative life. Prayers and study accompanied the education of the young monks and the daily tasks within the monastery. The days were regulated by an unchanging rhythm that was broken occasionally by solemn religious events and visits from important guests. The monastic

The colourful,
picturesque shop
signs decorate
the shops in
the village.

Rule of Saint Benedict had been scrupulously followed since the arrival of Robert de Torigny. The community — which consisted of the abbot, the monks and the novices — was dedicated to manual and intellectual tasks, as well as to charitable works. The level of comfort was minimal, in accordance with the monastery's rule. In time, however, thick, beautiful tapestries were hung on the walls to warm the freezing granite building, clothes became more luxurious and more comfortable, the simple fare gradually gave way to elaborate meals, and expensive furniture and objects filled the rooms. The visits from noble guests were certainly linked to these changes. New texts intended to reform the community life were applied to counteract this ostentatious display of luxury.

Like Saint-Jacques-de-Compostelle, Mont-Saint-Michel attracted many pilgrims, who travelled to the church on different roads; along the way they stayed at inns called *"sauvetés"*, which were founded by monasteries in the Middle Ages as sanctuaries. The final obstacle for all the pilgrims was to cross the bay. This is the origin of the medieval name for the mount, "Saint-Michel at Peril from the Sea". Yet the danger was not a sufficient deterrent and the prestige of Mont-Saint-Michel became greater year by year.

The dense row of shops and restaurants compete for attention along the only street of the village. Tourists and pilgrims started to return to Mont-Saint-Michel after it was restored in the late nineteenth century; it is now one of the most popular tourist destinations in France.

RESISTANCE

The Hundred Years' War between England and France created serious problems for the abbey. The revenues from all the properties owned by the abbey became increasingly hard to collect and Mont-Saint-Michel, standing between the two antagonists, hesitated in its allegiance. The residents resisted an attack by the English, who created a fortified outpost on Mont Tombelaine. A famous historical figure, Bertrand du Guesclin, took over the command of Mont-Saint-Michel and successfully resisted the invaders. While he carved a bloody path through enemy ranks, his wife,

Tiphaine, stayed at the mount, where she studied astrology.

After the defeat of the French army at Agincourt in 1415, Normandy once again became part of England, with the exception of Mont-Saint-Michel, where resistance was still strong. Betrayals and shifting alliances were standard practice in the Middle Ages: the abbot, Robert Jolivet, appeared to be preparing the defence of his abbey when he suddenly surrendered to the duke of Bedford, brother of King Henry V of England. He received his reward for his work (or betrayal), but the community at

Mont-Saint-Michel refused to acknowledge his act and retrenched behind the walls of the abbey. The English were determined to capture Mont-Saint-Michel and besieged the site in 1424, although without success, despite their impressive military arsenal. Yet they remained a threat. In 1434, the year of the final assault, most of the village of Mont-Saint-Michel was destroyed and the walls were breached in several places, but the *montois* (residents of Mont-Saint-Michel) resisted and even captured two English mortars, which still stand at the town gate.

After Charles VII recovered his realm, he travelled in 1448 to Rouen. Cardinal d'Estouteville, appointed abbot of Mont-Saint-Michel by the pope and later by the king, began to reconstruct the buildings left in ruins after the successive sieges.

The climb
up the many
staircases
to the top
is steep,
but the
Merveille
is more
than worth
the effort.

Above: Mont-Saint-Michel from the beach at Bec d'Andaine.
Opposite:
The Chapelle Saint-Aubert.
It was named after the virtuous founder of the mount and supposedly built on the site where an enormous megalith, which had blocked construction on the oratory at the top of the mount, landed after it was pushed off the top. According to legend, no one had been able to dislodge the stone; Saint Michael told Aubert that a certain baby could push it off with his tiny foot.

FROM MONASTERY TO FORTRESS

The damage was extensive: the collapsed Romanesque chancel in the abbey required repair, the walls had to be reconstructed and the village rebuilt. Construction of the Gothic chancel began in 1450 and continued, with interruptions, until 1521, when Abbot Jean de Lamps completed the work. A radical change in the everyday life of the abbey also appeared at this time. Charles VII transformed the rule by changing the status of the abbey. It was held in commendam, which meant that the abbot was a layman who could collect all the revenues from the abbey properties without necessarily living at Mont-Saint-Michel. With this began the decline of the monastic life, which was completely lax in the sixteenth century. The Rule of Saint Benedict was over: religious services were attended by a few old monks, while

Mère Poulard, a governess for the architect Édouard Corroyer, came with her employer to Mont-Saint-Michel where he was supervising the restoration of the abbey. After her marriage, she opened a restaurant that became famous for its omelets. Below: The Porte du Roi, which leads to the Grande Rue.

the younger brothers were hunting, dining or engaged in romantic pursuits.

Charles VII undertook much of the reconstruction work. His son Louis XI created the military order of Saint-Michel in honour of the heroic resistance against the English. During his second visit to Mont-Saint-Michel, he decided to construct dungeons, which transformed the purpose of the mount. He also added one of his favourite devices, an iron cage. It was in frequent use: François I employed the cage to permanently silence theologian Noël Béda, guilty of nothing more than criticising the king's foreign policy.

In the sixteenth century, the king's lieutenant, Gabriel du Puy, altered the defences of Mont-Saint-Michel by constructing a massive three-storey tower (the Tour Gabriel), which commanded a view over the vast stretch of sand. He also widened the ramparts to counter the range of incoming artillery fire. His work was soon put to the test during the Wars of Religion. Nine attempts were made to capture Mont-Saint-Michel, all of them unsuccessful. Protestant troops led by the fearsome Gabriel de Montgomery terrorised the towns around the abbey.

In the early seventeenth century, Mont-Saint-Michel was on the verge of material and moral bankruptcy. Most of the walls had fallen and some of the bays in the nave of the abbey had collapsed. The few remaining monks in the monastery were either very old or had no real religious faith. Members of the Saint Maur congregation were brought to Mont-Saint-Michel in 1622. The new occupants, imbued with religion and devout scholars, took charge of repairs to the abbey. They modified the architecture by remodelling the medieval parts of the buildings and by constructing a classical façade on the western side of the church.

The new monks, not satisfied
with reviving the spiritual life of the
abbey, then eased the suffering of
the prisoners who had been locked
up in cells or iron cages. Between
1685 and 1789, there were one hundred forty-seven incarcerations for
political reasons: publishing and
distributing pamphlets, Jansenism
and so forth. For these "banished"
prisoners, as they were called,
imprisonment in Mont-Saint-
Michel was a terrifying punish-
ment. Madame de Genlis recorded
in her memoirs that the under-
ground tunnels leading to the cells
were horribly dark, and that after
going down many staircases, she
reached a damp cave, which was a
sordid casket enclosing an abomina-
ble cage. Chavigny, a seventeenth-
century pamphleteer, occupied this
cage for thirteen years; when finally
liberated, he had, not surprisingly,
been driven completely mad.
Madame de Genlis continued her
account, writing that the young duc
de Chartres, future Louis-Philippe,
picked up an axe and made a sym-
bolic attempt to shatter the horrible
device invented by Cardinal Jean
Balu and installed by Louis XI.

THE "BASTILLE OF THE SEA"

The final twenty-five years of the
eighteenth century were catas-
trophic for Mont-Saint-Michel. In
1776, the belfry was struck by lightning for the twelfth time in its history. The damaged tower caved in
several bays in the Romanesque
nave; these were then torn down.

During the French Revolution,
the abbey was called the "Bastille
of the Sea". It was occupied by an
almost nonexistent community
which consisted of no more than a
dozen monks responsible for guard-
ing five prisoners. In 1790, all
church property was confiscated
and the monastic orders were abol-
ished. On 5 May 1790, the revolu-
tionaries demanded the property of
the abbey, and by the end of the
year its treasures were gone. In
1791, the bells were taken to Rouen

The Blackheaded
sheep of the salt
meadows. They
eat the grass that
grows around the
bay of Mont-Saint-
Michel. The meat
of these animals is
particularly
highly prized.

and melted down. All this took place in the middle of a civil war between royalists and republicans, a war which had put western France to fire and sword.

Following pages:
The Couesnon
River and views of
the Bay of
Mont-Saint-Michel.

The deserted abbey was renamed Mont Libre and used as a prison. There had never been so many monks and priests on the mount, even in the abbey's prime. Yet these six hundred churchmen, most of whom rejected the civil constitution, were behind bars, imprisoned in extremely difficult conditions. The shifting fortunes of the war meant that the Chouans (insurgents against the French Revolutionary Army) gained possession of Mont Libre for a short time; it was just long enough, however, to cut down the tree of Liberty planted at the top of the Tour Béatrix.

DECLINE AND FALL

The number of prisoners decreased and by 1778 only 200 remained. Common-law prisoners shared Mont-Saint-Michel with political prisoners, members of the Chouan movement and non-juring priests. By 1800, the abbey was empty and the only sign of activity was the Chappe telegraph, installed four years earlier.

The early nineteenth century was the lowest point in the long history of Mont-Saint-Michel. A Napoleonic

Fishing from the beach is an old tradition in the Bay of Mont-Saint-Michel. In the nineteenth century, the women collected cockles and shrimp, while the man fished for salmon, mullet and plaice.

decree made it an official prison. To accommodate the increasing number of internees, the buildings had to be transformed into workshops and dormitories. The abbey suffered severely in the process. An additional floor was built, and a partition was constructed along the width of the abbey. The stone slabs were removed so that the prisoners could not use them as weapons against the guards, and straw-weaving machines and looms were installed. Mont-Saint-Michel's fall from grace was complete. The final stroke was a fire, fed by the stockpiled cotton and straw, which destroyed the inside of the abbey church. Famous prisoners who "tasted" the damp straw of the cells — the euphemism used at the time to mean imprisonment — included Socialists Armand Barbès and Auguste Blanqui, who received extremely harsh treatment. Victor Hugo summed up the situation at Mont-Saint-Michel in 1836: "A sinister heap of cells, towers and rocks called Mont-Saint-Michel."

Napoleon III rendered null the first decree by signing a second one in 1863 which ended the existence of the district prison on Mont-Saint-Michel. Four years later, missionary priests of Saint-André-de-Pontigny moved to the mount.

Above: View of
Mont-Saint-Michel.
Right: The Logis
Tiphaine, or
Bertrand du
Guesclin house,
now a museum.

« HISTORICAL MONUMENT »

FINAL TRANSFORMATIONS
AND CONSOLIDATIONS

In 1874, Mont-Saint-Michel was classified as a Historical Monument. This decision, which seems obvious today, took many years. Prosper Mérimée, the influential inspector for the Monuments historiques (the French institution which governs state monuments), displayed no enthusiasm whatsoever after visiting Mont-Saint-Michel in 1841, writing that the Gothic architecture "looked horrible". Viollet-le-Duc, on the other hand, was a fervent admirer and praised the site: "No, it is impossible for us, men of the nineteenth century, to understand everything of beauty here. We are used to comfort, the pettiness of civilisation; we cannot look around us at these long ramparts battered on all sides by the sea, these walls pierced with small, windowless openings, these rocks that seem to slumber after such horrible convulsions, these uninhabited, roofless homes, black with smoke and time without feeling an involuntary shudder . . . Yet all this is in fact so great, and inspires such a beautiful and pensive sadness, that it is impossible to turn our backs on its nobility."

Even before it was classified, architect Édouard Corroyer had already started studying various restoration projects. The most urgent needs had to be met, which meant strengthening certain structures. Once the most important work was successfully taken care of, he then began the actual restoration, yet the results were less satisfying. Furthermore, he wanted to evict the people living on the ramparts and fiercely opposed the construction of the causeway connecting Mont-Saint-Michel to the mainland (although the work began under his supervision). He generated so much animosity that he was forced to leave his post. His debatable project for covering the cloister galleries with blue, yellow and ultramarine tiles created an uproar. Several years later, another architect, Paul Gout, thought he could correct the situation by laying down equally surprising red and black tiles. Finally, in 1962 a greenish schist roof re-established the architectural integrity of the building.

Victor Petitgrand succeeded Édouard Corroyer. Initially, he seemed to be more efficient and

more malleable, content to complete the work begun by his predecessor. The belfry and the abbey church still required renovation. He managed his project skilfully enough to gain approval for the neo-Gothic spire that has given Mont-Saint-Michel its tall graceful shape since last century. The chased copper statue of archangel Michael slaying the dragon, created by the sculptor Emmanuel Frémiet and installed on 6 August 1897, was the final touch in this overzealous yet necessary restoration.

VISITING MONT-SAINT-MICHEL

There is only one opening in the walls, the Porte de l'Avancée, which was constructed in the late sixteenth century. It leads to the Cour de l'Avancée and to the two other gates inside the walls. The first one, the Porte du Boulevard, was also built in the sixteenth century and leads to the fortified court

Left: The Salle des Hôtes where important guests were received. Above: One of the chapels. Mont-Saint-Michel has always been a religious site, except for brief periods in history. The Saint-Pierre Church is today the centre of pilgrimages to the mount.

of the same name. This court protects the fifteenth-century Porte du Roi, which has a drawbridge. Above this gate is the Logis du Roi. The Grande-Rue, the only street in the village, is lined with fifteenth- and sixteenth-century buildings. Some were constructed in stone, others with wonderful wooden facades. The parish church of Saint-Pierre (fifteenth and sixteenth centuries) contains several beautiful old statues. The Logis Thiphaine, or du Guesclin house, has been transformed into a museum. From here, visitors can climb up the Grand Degré, the main staircase leading to the abbey. The dark, steep Gouffre staircase, on the other hand, leads under a vaulted roof to the guardroom under the abbot's residence. From the guardroom, a passage leads to the church, the Aumônerie (Almshouse) and the Salle du Tribunal, known as the Salle de la Belle Chaise, where the abbot dispensed justice from a magnificently decorated throne.

To the west is the Chapelle Saint-Aubert — constructed in memory of the founder of Mont-Saint-Michel — the Fontaine Saint-Aubert and the Tour Gabriel.

The sober lines of the Romanesque nave form a striking contrast with the graceful arches of the triumphant Gothic chancel. The Romanesque nave now has only four bays with an arcade of arches, as the first bays collapsed and were removed. The Normandy-style nave was constructed in the eleventh century. The capitals were rebuilt in the nineteenth century. A gallery was constructed over the arches with an opening of two smaller arches over each bay. The top floor has narrow windows with semicircular arches. The spire, topped with a statue of Saint Michael, dates from the late nineteenth century; it replaced the Romanesque belfry constructed in 1136 by Abbot Bernard de Bec. The luminous Flamboyant Gothic chancel, reconstructed after the Romanesque chancel collapsed in 1421, is 25 metres high. The reconstruction project took almost a century to complete. The extraordinary height and luminosity was achieved through the use of an impressive arrangement of flying-buttresses on the outside. It is surrounded by an ambulatory which leads to nine chapels, each decorated with Renaissance bas-reliefs. Many windows were opened in the walls under the ribbed vaults, and clusters of small columns decorate each arch. One of the flying-buttresses forms a staircase which leads to the roof.

Fishing in the
plentiful
Couesnon River.

Known as the Escalier de Dentelle
(Lacework Staircase) because of the
carved balustrade, it climbs up over
the apse and leads to a gallery that
runs along the edge of the chancel
roof.

Three crypts support the weight
of the chancel: Notre-Dame-des-
Trente-Cierges, Saint-Martin and
the Crypte des Gros Piliers, the
most famous of the three. It defines
the size and layout of the chancel;
the enormous pillars in this crypt,
which measure 5 metres in circumference, form the foundations for
the structure above.

The Carolingian chapel, Notre-
Dame-sous-Terre, is the oldest
monument on Mont-Saint-Michel.
It was constructed on the site of the
first oratory. Successive construction projects gradually blocked off
all the doors and windows of this
chapel. The buildings to the north
and south of the church date from
the eleventh and twelfth centuries.
Part of the dormitory still remains
to the left of the façade; the room
has a wood-panelled barrel-vault
ceiling. The Promenoir des Moines
(Monk's Walk) is under this room.
The level just below the Promenoir
is the Crypte de l'Aquilon, the
former Aumônerie (Almshouse).
Nearby is the Chapelle Saint-
Étienne and the ossuary where a
large pulley was installed, used to
carry up food for the abbey.

The Merveille is the Gothic section of the abbey. The three-storey
construction includes, from the
bottom floor up, the Aumônerie,

the Salle des Hôtes (Guest Hall) and the Réfectoire (Refectory), all on the east side. To the west, also from the lowest level to the top, is the Cellier (Storeroom), the Salle des Chevaliers (Knights' Hall) and the Cloître (Cloisters). Pilgrims stayed in the Aumônerie, while the Salle des Hôtes was used for receptions given in honour of important guests. The monks generally ate in the refectory. The Salle des Chevaliers was the *scriptorium*. Constructed by Raoul de Villedieu in three years, from 1225 to 1228, the cloisters are considered the "Marvel of the Marvel", and seem to be suspended between the earth and the sky. Connected to the library where the manuscripts were kept, it is decorated with small columns grouped in clusters of five, which support arcades made from Caen limestone. Sculpted floral patterns decorate the arches.

Left: The chancel of the abbey church.
Opposite: A community of Benedictines returned to Mont-Saint-Michel in 1966.
Below: The monk's refectory at night.

ASTONISHING BEAUTY

The monument of Mont-Saint-Michel is an unbelievable labyrinth of structures which began with the Aubert oratory. A church with two naves was built over this oratory. The structure that we see today is a phenomenal achievement considering that the summit of Mont Tombe, where the 14-by-12-metre chapel was first built, was the foundation for an enormous architectural ensemble that rises close to 80 metres above sea level. Workers had to level the ground and find inven-

tive solutions to lay the foundations and construct a building on the sides collapsed in 1103.

The first construction materials used were stones from the mount itself. Although this was a practical solution, it had the serious disadvantage of reducing the constructible surface of an already small area. Rocks were then brought to Mont-Saint-Michel from the Chausay islands. The religious authorities were also forced to prohibit pilgrims from picking up bits of rock and carrying them off as precious relics.

King Philippe Auguste, who encouraged the fraternal dispute over Henry II's succession to England and Normandy, was also partly responsible for the siege and ensuing fire which engulfed Mont-Saint-Michel. Yet once he regained possession of the abbey, he contributed generously to its reconstruction. The new abbey, called "La Merveille" by awestruck pilgrims, was

Left: Model of the statue of Saint-Michael, sculpted by Emmanuel Frémiet for Victor Petitgrand and installed on top of the spire of the abbey church. Saint Michael symbolises the defender of the French nation, combatting its enemies personified by the dragon.
Above: Mont-Saint-Michel is a unique site for cultural events.

constructed during his reign. It was indeed an astonishing project: the Flamboyant Gothic cathedral (100 metres long, 20 metres wide and 40 metres high) stood on the rocky spur as if it had risen straight out of the sea.

Various other buildings were added to the southern side of the abbey in the thirteenth century and the first ramparts were constructed around the village. The Merveille then began to look like a feudal castle. When the defensive walls were strengthened by the Perrine and Châtelet towers, Mont-Saint-Michel became a real fortress.

The new chancel in the abbey church was completed in the sixteenth century. But the architectural history of Mont-Saint-Michel did not end with this project. The wave of cathedral-building which swept through Europe during the Middle Ages was over, but the Renaissance arrived and with it, a concern for the defence of the country's borders. The ramparts were extended and towers added along its length. The polygonal shape of the tower called the Tour Claudine was later adopted by the marquis de Vauban, charged by Louis XIV with making the fortresses of France impregnable.

In the Age of Enlightenment the congregation of Saint Maur made a few functional changes to the buildings. After the damage caused by lightning in 1776, they rebuilt the facade of the nave, which lost several bays in the disaster. This was severely criticised in the nineteenth century by architects who considered their contribution to be "hideous" and "a pitiful composition".

Yet today, despite the many renovation projects and combination of different styles, Mont-Saint-Michel is an example of perfect architectural integrity and magical harmony, as if some mysterious designer had the initial plan in mind all along.

Achevé d'imprimer en Espagne
Sur les presses de Fournier Artes Graficas, à Vitoria
ISBN : 2-83-070293-X
Dépôt légal : mai 1995